GENIUS BIOGRAPHIES

notionpress.com

GENIUS BIOGRAPHIES

ANKESH KOTHARI

notionpress.com

Notion Press

Old No. 38, New No. 6

McNichols Road, Chetpet

Chennai - 600 031

First Published by Notion Press 2016

ISBN 978-93-5206-975-0

The Stories that Need Telling

"I only tell stories, Your Grace. They may be truths, they may be fictions. All I know is that the stories themselves exist and that I must tell them."

– Hoid (Warbreaker)

– Brandon Sanderson

This book contains stories of geniuses: folks who have reached the top of their fields in science and politics and sports and business and war and entertainment.

I have tried to make sure that these are accurate stories. But full disclosure: I've not met any of these geniuses. It's based on second hand research.

But the stories needed telling. And so here they are. Hope they help motivate you and teach you a few tricks that can make your climb to the top easier.

– Ankesh Kothari

(Student of the masters)

CONTENTS

Why Should You Read Genius Biographies?

The Story of the Rise of Great Britain

In the fifteenth century, England was in a crisis. The society had stagnated. The economy was in a recession, and the country was torn by a civil war that had lasted for decades.

Finally, in 1485, Henry Tudor engaged Richard III—the then king of England—in battle and won.

Coincidentally, in 1485, William Caxton, the first person to run a printing press in England, published Le Morte D'Arthur—the story of King Arthur and his knights of the roundtable in English.

Henry Tudor was heavily inspired by the legend of King Arthur and his gallant knights. In fact, he was so obsessed by the story that he "traced" his ancestry all the way back to King Arthur, and named his firstborn son Arthur.

Henry took King Arthur as a model of how heroic kings should behave. He invested in creating policies that bring economic prosperity and peace. He formed the Court of Star Chamber to provide swift justice and resolve disputes. And, he subsidized shipbuilding so that England could strengthen its navy and become powerful again.

As a result, Henry Tudor was the last king of England to win his throne on the battlefield. Henry Tudor brought the end of the Middle Ages in England and put in the foundation that helped England conquer a large part of the world.

But Who Wrote the Story of King Arthur?

In 1451, Thomas Malory was rotting in prison. But, he was lucky to be in a prison that was adjacent to a monastery because prisoners were allowed to borrow and read books from the library in the monastery.

Thomas started reading an old book by a Welsh monk named Geoffrey of Monmouth: "The History of the Kings of Britain." Taking notes from that book, and adding a few more tales from other French poets and writers, Thomas began to write his own book on King Arthur: Le Morte D'Arthur.

This was the book that inspired King Henry to make Britain great again. But here is the twist: not one word of the story of King Arthur was true!

Historians couldn't find a single trace of King Arthur. Geoffrey of Monmouth made it all up, and Thomas Malory embellished it further. But it was still the biography that inspired a king to start building an empire.

Action Summary:

* If fake biographies and stories can inspire and lead to the building of the biggest empire the world has ever seen, imagine what real biographies of real geniuses can do...
* Read this book with an open mind. Take notes. And implement the ideas and strategies that you learn.

Before we begin...

You can receive more “Genius Biographies” not covered in this book by subscribing to the email newsletter:

http://GeniusBiographies.com/subscribe/

Abraham Lincoln

The Unique Strategy Abe Lincoln Used to Win an Election

In the year 1860, the Republican Party in United States had to select their presidential nominee.

Everyone thought that William Seward—the senator from New York—would win the nomination with ease. He was the most popular candidate by far.

There were a few other candidates too. Notable amongst them were Edward Bates of Missouri and Salmon Chase of Ohio. One relatively unknown candidate from Illinois joined the race too: Abraham Lincoln.

Lincoln's Strategy to Outsmart His More Popular Competitors

Lincoln knew that he won't be able to become the favorite choice of the majority of the delegates. Many delegates were too loyal to Seward, Bates and Chase already. But Lincoln also knew that no candidate had more than 50% backing of the delegates.

So Lincoln decided on a strategy to become the number two choice of the highest number of delegates!

His strategy was to give offense to no one. He wanted to leave the delegates "in the mood to come to us, if they shall be compelled to give up their first love."

So while Seward, Bates and Chase concentrated only on their core constituency, Lincoln traveled the country—willing to go anywhere to give speeches.

For example, when Seward was on a trip to Europe and Cooper Union in New York was looking for a Republican to give a speech to its audience, Salmon Chase declined the invitation thinking that he could make no in-roads in New York—Seward's state. But Abraham Lincoln jumped on the chance in a jiffy!

How Does the Strategy Fare During Nomination?

It was May 18, 1960—the day when Republican delegates nominated their presidential candidate. A candidate required at least 233 votes to win. In the first round, the results were the following:

- Seward: 173½ votes
- Lincoln: 102 votes
- Chase: 49 votes
- Bates: 48 votes

Seward had the lead with a very good margin. But things changed quickly during the second round when people started changing their votes to select one sole winner.

In Round 2, Seward received 184½ votes—hardly moving ahead. But Lincoln made huge strides and received 181 votes—only 3½ votes behind Seward.

Both Chase and Bates lost ground and the match was now between Seward and Lincoln alone.

But over the years, Seward made quite a few enemies. And not many people liked him outside his core constituency. On the other hand, Lincoln had spent a lot of time making sure that he was the number two choice of the majority of the delegates. Hence, in Round 3, Lincoln quickly gained the lead and crossed 233 votes to become nominated as the Republican Presidential candidate!

Action Summary:

- If the competition is stiff, and you're not the first one on the scene, then instead of trying to become the number one choice of people, position yourself to become the best number two choice out there.
- People love an underdog. It doesn't take much to go from being number two to number one if you've not offended a lot of people.

Alexander the Great

How Alexander Actually Became Alexander the Great

Alexander came to his throne at the ripe young age of twenty when his father Philip of Macedon passed away. Being extremely ambitious, Alexander started a military campaign right away. Over the next few years, he conquered the Balkans, Turkey, Syria, Jerusalem, and Egypt. And then, he decided to attack the mighty Persian Empire.

Alexander started by attacking and conquering the smaller Persian Satraps. After a few such skirmishes and battles, Darius—the king of Persia—decided to swat Alexander out of Persia. He gathered a huge army of more than 100,000 soldiers and marched on.

Alexander Versus Darius

Darius actually surprised Alexander. Instead of attacking Alexander head on with a massive army, Darius marched behind Alexander's command line and cut off his supply. Alexander had no choice but to countermarch and face Darius. It was suicide, as Alexander only had 40,000 soldiers. Darius had better equipment and weaponry than Alexander—more horses and chariots too.

How Did Alexander Win against the Overwhelming Persian Forces?

Even Alexander's generals feared the upcoming war—predicting it would be a blood bath.

Alexander realized that it would be very hard to win against the Persian army. It was just too big. So Alexander gave just one simple order to his soldiers:

Kill Darius

Every soldier in Alexander's force had one clear mission, one clear target: Darius. They didn't have to beat the entire Persian army. They just had to kill one target. As soon as the war began, they went after that one target in full force.

Their focus took the Persian wing that protected Darius by surprise, and Darius soon realized what Alexander was up to. He fled to save his life. Seeing their commander and king run away, the other generals and soldiers fled too.

And Alexander, with poor equipment and outnumbered soldiers, won against the mighty Persians.

Alexander became "Alexander the Great."

Action Summary:

- Focus.
- You can take on much bigger competitors if you focus all your energy into something they are weak at.

Bruce Lee

How Bruce Lee Becomes One of the Best Fighters the World Has Ever Seen

Bruce Lee was a brat as a kid. He constantly got into fights. He had to transfer schools because of his poor conduct. His academic performance was pretty dismal too.

After one fight too many, when thirteen-year-old Bruce Lee came home bloodied, his father enrolled him into "Wing Chun" martial arts school.

Wing Chun was a type of martial arts that doesn't rely on one's size or strength. Instead it focused on proper balanced stance, so that one could either deflect or redirect external attacks. It emphasized close range combat and aimed to disarm and silence the opponent as quickly as possible.

Yip Man—Bruce Lee's martial arts teacher—encouraged his students to take part in organized fight competitions in the hope that they won't get into street fights.

Bruce Lee excelled under Yip Man. And when he moved to United States, he started his own martial arts training school at the age of nineteen.

Bruce Lee Versus Wong Jack Man

A few years later, the Chinese community in California issued Bruce Lee a warning not to teach and reveal the secrets of Chinese martial arts to people who were not

Chinese themselves. When Bruce Lee declined, a fight was organized between him and Wong Jack Man. If Bruce Lee won the fight, he could teach whomever he wanted. But if he lost, he had to stop teaching people who were not Chinese.

Wong Jack Man was a proficient martial arts teacher himself. He excelled in Tai Chi as well as Northern Shaolin forms of martial arts.

Tai Chi was a slow and soft martial art. People were taught not to directly fight with brute force but to exhaust the opponent and slow him down. Northern Shaolin was a type of kung fu that emphasized long range fighting, quickly attacking and retreating away.

On the scheduled date, Bruce Lee came ready to fight with Wong Jack Man. And it was one of the most frustrating fights Bruce Lee had ever fought.

Because while Bruce Lee's Wing Chun technique focused on close combat fighting, Wong Jack Man's Northern Shaolin technique was more about hit and run. While Bruce Lee went for quickness, Wong Jack Man aimed for slowing the pace down.

The Epiphany That Led to a New Martial Arts System

In the end, Bruce Lee won the long hard fight. But not before it gave him an epiphany. Before the fight, Bruce Lee was content in mastering Wing Chun. But after the fight, he realized that he needed different tools for different tasks.

He started dissecting other martial arts and learnt their best techniques. He also dissected western fighting techniques like boxing and fencing and adapted their best ideas to martial arts.

This effort led Bruce Lee to create his own hybrid martial arts system: "Jeet Kune Do." A style of fighting without style, having no fixed patterns or methods.

Having the best attack and defense moves from various martial arts, without having the limitations of any single one of them, made Bruce Lee one of the best fighters the world had ever seen!

Action Summary:

- Don't limit yourself. Take good ideas from everyone and tweak them to make it your own.
- Adapt. As Bruce Lee says: "Empty your mind, be formless, shapeless, like water. If you put water into a cup, it becomes the cup. You put water into a bottle and it becomes the bottle. You put it in a teapot it becomes the teapot. That water can flow, or it can crash. Be water my friend."

Kenneth Cole

The Reason Why Kenneth Cole Makes a Movie

Kenneth Cole was the founder of one of the biggest fashion companies in the world. Kenneth Cole's fashion acumen was renowned all over. But what most people didn't know about him was his go-getter attitude.

Kenneth Cole's father—Charles Cole—owned the El Greco shoe manufacturing company. Kenneth joined his father's business right after college and started to learn the ropes. In 1982, he ventured on his own and began his own business: Kenneth Cole Incorporated.

The Grim Beginnings of Kenneth Cole Incorporated

In his over enthusiasm, Kenneth manufactured 40,000 pairs of shoes. But then, he found it hard to sell them. Kenneth couldn't afford to rent a commercial space in Manhattan, and so he settled on selling shoes to other retailers and distributors. But sales were very slow.

When Kenneth heard that Market Week was being organized at the Hilton Hotel in New York, he saw a ray of hope. Market Week was an event where all the big fashion wholesalers and volume retailers came together. One big sale over there would solve Kenneth's problems. But Kenneth found that renting a showroom to exhibit his shoes during Market Week was out of his budget too.

So Kenneth decided to simply hire a truck, park it two blocks away from the Hilton Hotel, and exhibit his shoes there.

But there was more bad luck. When Kenneth went to the mayor's office to get permission to park his truck, he was told that permits were only given to utility companies to perform city maintenance and production companies to shoot movies. No one else could get a permit.

The Birth of a Movie Production Company

And so Kenneth hatched a plan. He quickly renamed his company to Kenneth Cole Productions and applied for a permit to shoot a full-length motion picture called "The Birth of a Shoe Company."

Kenneth upgraded his truck to a forty-foot trailer, hired a cameraman, and got some actresses to act as female models who would sell the shoes. He added red velvet ropes outside the trailer, and only allowed a limited number of people to enter at one time.

Within two and a half days, Kenneth ended up selling all of his forty thousand pair of shoes! And his company was on its way to expand and grow.

Even today, the company is called Kenneth Cole Productions, Inc—to honor the beginnings of the company as a movie studio!

Action Summary:

- Hustle. Do what you need to do to succeed, using whatever resources at hand.
- Go where your audience hangs out to sell.

Oprah Winfrey

The Single Thing That Helped an Abused Oprah Rise up from the Poverty Mindset

Oprah Winfrey had an upbringing harder than we could imagine.

She was born in a small town in Mississippi to Vernita Lee—a housemaid—who couldn't even afford to feed her young baby. Oprah was promptly sent to her grandmother to be taken care of, who beat her with a stick for the smallest of mistakes. At school, Oprah was constantly teased for being poor and wearing potato sacks as clothes.

If that weren't enough, at nine, Oprah was molested by multiple men who were close to her—her uncle, her cousin, and a close friend of the family. After four years of abuse, she finally ran away. But within a year, she became pregnant. Only for her newborn son to die shortly after birth—leading to a bout of depression.

Oprah Pivots Her Life

After the tragic death of her son, Oprah finally went to Nashville to stay with whom she believed was her father: Vernon Winfrey. Vernon Winfrey was a tough disciplinarian. Though he wasn't Oprah's biological father, he took her in and gave her a secure home and he let her believe for years that he was in fact her father.

With some discipline and some encouragement, Vernon made Oprah's education her primary focus. Oprah became an honors student. She also joined her high school speech team and won an oratory contest—the rest is now history.

The Secret Ingredient that Helps Oprah Change Her Mindset

But there was one more thing that Vernon did that changed Oprah. He enabled her to rise up from the poverty mindset. Vernon required Oprah to read one book and write a report on it every week.

Books freed Oprah from the invisible mental shackles. Books gave her ambition. Books showed her what was possible.

Action Summary:

* Read good books regularly. Because books are the shortcut to help you expand your mind.

Theodore Roosevelt

How Theodore Roosevelt Becomes Superman

Theodore Roosevelt was born as a sickly child in the year 1858. He suffered from severe asthma. Asthma was not very well understood in the year 1858. To treat his coughing and respiratory problems, Roosevelt was taken to a lot of doctors who prescribed all sorts of remedies.

Some recommended a vacation to hill stations. Others recommended drinking coffee or whiskey. One doctor even recommended smoking cigars. Most of these remedies made Roosevelt's asthma worse than before.

Besides asthma, Roosevelt also suffered from headaches and abdominal pains. He couldn't go to regular school or play with other children. Roosevelt spent most of his time at home reading books or talking with his father. The only outdoor activity he enjoyed was going for midnight carriage rides with his father once in a while.

The Conversation That Builds Conviction

While Roosevelt's father loved him deeply, he was a bit dismayed with having a son who was sick all the time. When Roosevelt was twelve years old, one conversation he had with his father resolved his attitude and changed his life. His father told him: "Theodore you have the mind but you have not the body, and without the help of the body the mind cannot go as far as it should."

To which Roosevelt instantly replied: "I will make my body."

Making of the Body

Roosevelt started pushing himself to be in a slightly better physical state than the day before. With the help of his father, he built a gym in his home where he could start lifting weights and building strength. He started hiking even though it affected his asthma. Later on, he also started climbing mountains even though the weather was cold and the air was thin.

When he entered college, he took up rowing and boxing—two sports that challenge one's body. After graduation, his doctor advised him to take a desk job and avoid strenuous activity because of a weak heart. Instead Roosevelt got married and climbed the Matterhorn Mountain on the border of Italy and Switzerland with his wife during his honeymoon!

The Assassination Attempt

One occasion in 1912 marked the heights of Roosevelt's willpower and strength. During campaigning, he got up to give a speech at a podium when John Schrank shot him because he opposed the President's ability to seek a third term.

Fortunately, the bullet hit Roosevelt's steel eyeglass case and the fifty pages of speech he had prepared before it lodged into his body. This slowed the bullet down and prevented it from penetrating his lungs or heart. While any sane person would go straight to the hospital, Roosevelt rejected the notion and instead started with his speech as scheduled.

His opening remarks:

"Friends... I don't know whether you fully understand that I have just been shot; but it takes more than that to kill a Bull Moose... The bullet is in me now, so that I cannot make a very long speech, but I will try my best."

Roosevelt went on to speak for ninety minutes!

Action Summary:

* Without the body, the mind cannot go as far. Optimize your health first and foremost.
* Push yourself to become just slightly better than yesterday. Overcome your weaknesses slowly but steadily.

John D. Rockefeller

How John D. Rockefeller Becomes a Billionaire

John D. Rockefeller was the first billionaire the world had ever seen. When he was young and earning fifty cents a day as an accountant, he made two goals for himself:

1. To make $100,000.
2. To live till 100.

While he missed his age goal by three years and died at age ninety-seven, he overshot his money ambition by four big zeroes. But what made him so successful?

Devout Eliza and Devil Bill

Rockefeller was the second of six children born to Eliza and Bill Rockefeller. Bill was a charmer and while he started out as a lumberjack, he soon found that he was pretty good with sales. So, he became a botanic physician and went from town to town selling "elixirs"—herbs that would heal everything from common cold to cancer. Even though Bill was a conman, people loved being around him. Neighbors soon started calling him "Devil Bill."

On the other hand, Rockefeller's mother Eliza was a devout Baptist. She was honest and hardworking and taught all her kids how to act responsibly from a young age. Rockefeller started raising turkey and selling potatoes to earn some money from a very young age because of his mother's influence.

Rockefeller borrowed the best traits from both his parents. He learnt the art of deal making from his father who would often persuade and cheat his own kids to give him their money. Bill often advised his kids to "trade dishes for platter" and to look for the better part of a deal.

And from his mother, Rockefeller learnt thriftiness and charity. His mother's motto was "willful waste makes woeful want." But even though, she was poor, she often tithed to the church. From a very young age, Rockefeller started keeping a personal daily accounts book where he kept track of each penny he earned and spent. And from his first paycheck, Rockefeller started tithing exactly 10% of his income to his church.

Side note: The Money Tracking Ritual

Nelson Rockefeller—John D. Rockefeller's grandson—told the story of how keeping track of money had ritualized in the Rockefeller family. Rockefeller taught his son John Jr., who taught his son Nelson, to keep a daily accounts diary from a very young age. All the kids were required to save 10% of their money, give 10% of their income to charity, and account for the rest. Because of this ritual, Rockefellers had managed to not lose their fortunes even after five and six generations.

The Standard Oil Strategy

While John D. Rockefeller started as an accountant, he didn't remain one for long. In 1859, at the age of twenty, he along with a partner—Maurice Clark—raised $4,000 and went into the production business. They did very well and in 1863, with the help of a chemist—Samuel

Andrews—built a small oil refinery. In 1865, Rockefeller raised $72,500 and bought his partner Clark's stake to become the majority shareholder. In 1870, the company name was changed to Standard Oil.

Rockefeller always kept a sharp eye on costs. But the real benefits came when he implemented his mother's motto for the oil business. Their refinery was the first one that focused on re-using and monetizing the by-products and waste. Standard Oil refineries became the most efficient in the industry because of this thriftiness.

In 1871, Rockefeller took a page from his father's notebook. He made a deal with the railroads and formed a cartel through which Standard Oil received steep rebates for shipping. Their shipping costs were as much as 50% less than their competitors.

With these two tools in his arsenal, Rockefeller went on to dominate the business world.

The Cleveland Massacre

1. Rockefeller improved his factories efficiency levels and kept a sharp eye on costs
2. Rockefeller then went and negotiated to get preferential shipping rates
3. By being thrifty and negotiating steep discounts, he could slash his prices to a level where the competitor could no longer make a profit
4. He then raised investment pools to buy these competitors out

In less than four months in 1872, Rockefeller used the above four pronged approach to buy out twenty-two of his twenty-six rivals in Cleveland. This episode later came to be known as the "Cleveland Massacre."

By being the most efficient operator and the shrewdest negotiator, Rockefeller made the Standard Oil grow into the biggest company in the world. Standard Oil started manufacturing as many as 300 oil-based products: everything from paint to Vaseline to chewing gum. At its peak, Standard Oil owned 20,000 oil wells and employed over 100,000 people!

Rockefeller became so successful in creating his monopoly that special laws had to be passed to put breaks on his ambition and to make sure competition thrived in the marketplace.

In 1911, Standard Oil was broken down into smaller companies. Its children companies are still one of the biggest companies in the world: BP, ExxonMobil, Chevron, Amoco, Pennzoil.

Action Summary:

* Learn to be thrifty. Keep a track of all your income and expenses. And focus on becoming more efficient than others.
* Learn the art of negotiation and deal making.
* It's a good rule to save 10% of your income, donate 10%, and live on the rest.

Tiger Woods

Tiger Woods' Secret to Dominating Golf

Eldrick "Tiger" Woods took the world of Golf by storm in 1996. He was a young nineteen-year-old guy who kept on winning championship after championship and breaking records after records. For almost six years, there was no stopping Tiger Woods.

But in 2002, other golfers finally started catching up. While Tiger Woods was still winning tournaments, his skills had reached a plateau. Other golfers started giving him a run for his money.

Going from Bad to Worse

And then, things went from bad to worse. In 2003 and 2004, Tiger didn't win a single major tournament. Other golfers were now consistently beating him. And critics were already writing Tiger Woods off.

But things were completely different behind the scenes. When the world saw Tiger Woods go from bad to worse, he was in fact becoming better and better.

Fixing the Problem

In 2002, when Tiger realized that he had hit a plateau, he started analyzing the reason and realized that while his swing was awesome, it was too upright and did not have room for improvement. It was holding him back. So he promptly replaced his old coach Butch Harmon with Hank Haney, who was a swing expert.

It however took Tiger a long time to unlearn his upright swing and master the new flatter swing. It was during this transition phase that Tiger didn't win any major tournaments.

But once he had perfected the new swing, things changed very quickly. The new swing consistently gave Tiger a 20–30 yard advantage which enabled him to win eleven tournaments in 2005!

Action Summary:

- Sometimes, becoming better means you have to unlearn your old habits.
- Have patience and strong will power to deal with the bad patches you have to go through to becoming better.
- Learn from the best teachers and coaches you can find.

Charles Darwin

Charles Darwin Publishes His Theory of Evolution

Instead of being considered one of the foremost scientists of his era, Charles Darwin was close to being a footnote in a science textbook somewhere.

Darwin came upon his theory of evolution when he spent five weeks at the Galapagos Islands in 1835. The Galapagos was a group of small islands that were 50–60 miles apart from each other. But all of these islands were formed from the same rock, and under similar climate conditions. And yet, the tortoises differed from island to island. Minor change in circumstances over long periods of time led to slight changes in the same animal on different islands.

Theory of Evolution Versus Divine Creation

Darwin realized that this disproved the prevalent theory that species were individually created or that species were transmuted from one animal to another—most likely by a divine power. But Darwin kept quiet about his thoughts. He was afraid what his Victorian peers would think of him. After his marriage, he was troubled about what his extremely pious wife would make of his theory of natural selection.

It got so bad that anytime he even thought of publishing his thoughts, he had anxiety attacks. He wrote to a friend that he couldn't publish his theory because it was "like confessing to a murder."

The Big Nudge

Twenty-three years passed and Darwin had still not published his theory. He would talk about it now and then with a few scientist friends, but he just could not write and publish it for wider readership.

That was until he read an essay from Alfred Russell Wallace in 1858, which spoke about a similar theory. This forced Darwin to sit down and write his book "On the origin of species" and publish it in 1859.

If it wasn't for the nudge that Alfred Russell Wallace's essay gave him, Darwin would have been a footnote today just because he feared disapproval.

Action Summary:

- Don't allow peer pressure to rule your actions. Don't let the fear of hurting your social standings stop you from taking action.
- Competition is good. It makes you better. It spurs you to act quicker. Be proactive in looking out for healthy competition.

Louis CK

How Louis CK Jump Starts a Stalled Career

It was 1985 and eighteen-year-old Louis Székely went to an open night at a comedy club in Boston. He was given five minutes of time to perform. But he bombed badly and quit in just two minutes. The whole experience was so bad that it put off Louis to even try to perform stand up comedy again for two whole years!

But the yearning to become a comedian was strong. So after a couple of years, Louis tried again. He adopted the stage name of Louis CK and started practicing. Slowly but surely, he started performing better at other comedy clubs. Soon he started receiving paid gigs and he got to open for big name comedians like Jerry Seinfeld.

Hitting the Plateau

He parlayed that into writing for comedy shows for David Letterman and Chris Rock. And occasionally, he performed for shows such as Late Show with David Letterman, and The Tonight Show with Jay Leno.

But that was where his career stalled. More than a decade went by and Louis found himself in the same circles doing the same things. His fame stopped increasing and new opportunities became sparse.

The Crazy Strategy that Helps Him Overcome the Plateau

That was when he heard an interview by the comedy legend George Carlin that changed things. In that interview, George Carlin said that he recorded a comedy special every year. And after the recording, he threw away all those jokes and never used them again and started writing anew.

Initially, Louis thought that this was crazy. It took years of practice for a comedian to make up one solid hour of jokes that don't bomb. How could he just throw away all those jokes that had a track record of doing well?

But soon Louis realized: George Carlin's set became better year after year. Not only were the jokes fresh, they were funnier too. And so, Louis decided to try the same thing: did a comedy special every year and never repeated the jokes from that special.

Within a couple of years of doing this, Louis found that he had improved tremendously as a comedian too. And others had started taking notice. He soon got his own TV show. Comedy Central listed him in top 100 funniest stand-ups of all time and Louis CK became really, really famous with a very loyal fan base.

In 2013, Louis released his stand-up special "Oh My God" on his website without the help of big distributors. He still does over $16 million of sales!

Action Summary:

* Practice hard to become better.
* Learn from the masters who have already achieved the success you are seeking. Read interviews and success stories. Find your own mentors.
* Keep on working on new material. Out innovate yourself. Your aim should be to make your past-self obsolete every year—before anyone else does.

Joe Girard

Joe Girard Becomes the World's Greatest Salesman

Joe Girard was born during the depression in one of the most deplorable ghettos in Detroit city. Joe had a difficult relationship with his father. At a very young age, Joe started shining shoes of people in saloons. He had a tough childhood. Even though Joe came from a poor background and had a hard start, he became really successful.

How Successful did Joe Become?

The Guinness Book of World Records listed Joe Girard as the "World's Greatest Retail Salesman" for twelve consecutive years.

People actually used to lineup to meet Joe, so that he could sell them cars. There would always be a queue in front of Joe Girard's dealership on every Saturday morning. Joe Girard sold more cars individually than most dealers sell in total. He sold an average of six cars every day, throughout his selling career. He sold 13,001 cars during his selling career... every one of them at retail.

The Simple Secret

Joe managed to sell so many cars because he built and maintained relationships. Joe used to send thirteen cards to all his prospects and clients every year: one every month and one for Christmas. He created a place for himself in the brains of his prospects and clients by keeping in touch with them.

He made sure that he was in peoples' minds when they had to buy a car. And that was how he sold six cars a day, every day.

Joe Girard followed up with his clients even when there was no reason to.

Action Summary:

- Keep in touch with people regularly.
- Send them "Thank you" notes.
- Send them season's greetings.
- Send them news and information that will be beneficial to them.
- Send them free goodies.

Dorothy Parker

The Chutzpah Dorothy Parker Uses to Get Her Start in Life

Dorothy Parker was known for her wit and her melancholy. She wrote with precision and her poems and short stories made her famous. But she was also unhappy a lot and made quite a few suicide attempts throughout her life.

Dorothy's mother passed away when Dorothy was just four years old. Dorothy was the youngest of four children but she was never close to any of her siblings. Her father was physically abusive to her. And when he remarried, Dorothy hated her new step mother because she was a devout Catholic and forced Dorothy to go to a stuffy Catholic school.

When Dorothy was twenty years old, her father passed away. Because his estate was divided between all the siblings, not much was left for Dorothy. To earn a living, she started playing piano at a dancing school. In her spare time, she would sit and write.

Dorothy sent quite a few of her poems and verses to various magazines and publications. And she collected a big pile of rejection letters. While this did make her doubt if she was any good, she never lost her confidence that she would make it big. And in the end, that had made all the difference.

First Publication

When Dorothy was twenty-one years old, her poem "Any Porch" was finally accepted by Frank Crowninshield—the editor of Vanity Fair. Along with the acceptance letter, Dorothy also received a check for $12.

Dorothy marched down to Vanity Fair's office and asked to be seen by Frank Crowninshield. When he met her, Dorothy proposed that because he had liked her poem he might give her a job as well.

Frank refused because there was no opening at Vanity Fair. But he liked Dorothy's confidence and chutzpah. And when there was an opening at Vogue—Vanity Fair's sister publication—he remembered Dorothy and offered it to her.

The entry level job was the beginning of a fantastic literary career. Dorothy made her mark and quickly rose up the ranks because of her crisp and witty writing. But it wouldn't have been possible if she hadn't gone and asked for a job in the first place!

Action Summary:

- Every one doubts themselves now and then. But don't let that wither your confidence.
- Ask. Ask for what you want. You'll be surprised as to how many times you will receive it.

Colonel Harland Sanders

How Colonel Sanders Makes His Fortune and Builds KFC after Retirement

Harland Sanders suffered from one of the worst diseases one could face. He was never happy with what he had. He always found the grass greener on the other side. And as a result, he chased all sorts of get rich quick schemes that never made him rich.

Sanders started working as a blacksmith's help at Sheffield, Alabama when he was sixteen years old. But within a year, he joined to become a fireman at a railroad at Jasper, Alabama.

A couple of years later, he joined another railroad company in Jackson, Tennessee, but this time as a laborer. And during night time, he started studying law through correspondence. Once he became a lawyer, he moved again to Little Rock and started his law practice.

He did that for three years. Before he quit law, he moved again to Jeffersonville and became an insurance salesman. After being fired for insubordination, he moved cities once more—this time to Louisville and started selling insurance there.

Becoming an Entrepreneur

After a couple of years of that, he stopped selling insurance and started his own business. He raised money to buy a boat and started a ferry service on the Ohio River between Jefferson and Louisville. And even though the ferry service was doing really well, Sanders sold his stake for $22,000 and started a new company manufacturing acetylene lamps.

The venture failed when another company started selling electric lamps on credit. So he then moved to Winchester, Kentucky and became a salesman for the Michelin tire company. When Michelin shut one of their plants down, Sanders lost his sales job.

He moved to Nicholasville, Kentucky and started running a Standard Oil service station. He stuck there for a few years, before moving to Corbin, Kentucky to run a service station for Shell Oil.

The Chicken Innovation

To increase his income, he started serving chicken dishes to travelers who came to fill gas at his service station. Because he didn't have a restaurant, he served the diners at his living quarters next door. Sanders developed a way to fry the chicken in a pressure cooker instead of a frying pan, which reduced the time to cook chicken from thirty minutes to nine minutes. Because of which he could serve his diners a lot quicker!

After nine years, Sanders bought a motel in Ashville, Tennessee. But then World War II started, gas became rationed, and so Sanders had to shut down his motel as travelers dried up.

The next couple of years, he traveled to Seattle and back to Tennessee working in various cafeterias.

He finally just set up a 140 seats restaurant in Corbin, Kentucky again and started selling chicken there. As luck would have it, Pete Harman of Salt Lake City loved his chicken and Sanders managed to sell the first Kentucky Fried Chicken franchise to him in 1952. No upfront money, but Harman would give Sanders five cents for every chicken sold.

The Doom that Forced Sanders to Focus

In 1955, a new interstate highway was built that bypasses Corbin. As a result, business dried up. Sanders was forced to sell out at a loss. And he found himself sixty-five years old and penniless.

The only thing working for Sanders was the $105 he received from social security and the little bit of royalty he earned from Pete Harman. So Sanders decided to hit the road and convince more restaurants to franchise his chicken. But for the first time in his life—maybe because he had hit the retirement age—he decided that he would do nothing but sell the chicken franchise. He won't divert his attention to other ventures and ideas.

He started driving from town to town with a pressure cooker. He would enter a restaurant and challenge the owner: "I bet my chicken will taste better than yours." If the owner liked the chicken, and the quick way Sanders cooked it, he would license it for five cents per chicken.

Sanders stuck to this though, initially, he heard a lot more nos than yeses. Legend has it that 1009 restaurants refused Sanders. But because he stuck to the plan, by 1964, he had 600 franchises on board and could sell his business for $2 million and retire!

Action Summary:

- Stick to one thing. You can make the grass greener on your side by cultivating it over a long period.
- Once you have a proven product, then scaling up is a numbers game. You will hear No a lot of times, but don't let that disappoint you.

Paris Hilton

Why is Paris Hilton Famous?

When most people were asked why Paris Hilton was famous? People replied with a quip: she was famous for being famous. But was that all there was to her? How did she manage to become a model and an actress? How she had her own reality TV show, had her own line of clothes and perfumes, owned a motorcycle racing team and became a DJ that played in Ibiza's best night clubs, on top of being a brand ambassador for various brands?

Paris Hilton was the great granddaughter of Conrad Hilton—the founder of Hilton Hotels—and had inherited a small fortune. She was a bit spoilt during her childhood and was expelled from her school the month she turned eighteen. But she didn't let that stop her from becoming a model and a socialite at the top of the pecking order in New York.

The Sex Tape Fame

Paris became a household name when her infamous sex tape was leaked on Internet in 2003. The video hit schadenfreude motherlode. Human nature being what it is, people derived pleasure from Paris's misfortune and there was nothing to stop the sex tape from going viral.

Paris became a paparazzi favorite overnight. Reporters followed her everywhere and dug into every small detail of her life. To control the damage to her image, Paris hired a publicist.

Paris Hilton's Strategy to Leverage Fame to Gain More Fame

The publicist did a damn good job. Paris made it to "Sexiest Women" lists in various magazines like FHM and Maxim. She routinely made it to Page 6 too. And even after being so infamous, she started receiving celebrity endorsement deals.

While most people would find it impossible to rise above their infamy, Paris thrived. And that's because she had a secret strategy. Even when she was featured on Page 6 and interviewed by various magazines, she didn't talk about herself instead she talked about other people and other brands. She spoke about the restaurants she craved, the designer clothes she wore, the DJ she loved, and who made her dog's sweater. She dropped names and focused attention on other brands.

Seriously, have you ever seen a Paris Hilton interview where she hadn't mentioned other brands or people? It didn't take long for people to realize that Paris Hilton was a walking billboard. She gave attention to them and so they started giving attention to her. Fame begets more fame.

Action Summary:

- Give to get.
- Focus attention on other people, and they will want to make sure the spotlight remains on you.

FREDDIE ROACH

Freddie Roach Becomes the Best Boxing Coach

Freddie Roach started to learn boxing when he was just six years old—mainly because his elder brother boxes. But he was never very enthusiastic about it. When he was fifteen years old, his mother asked him: "Why do you fight anyways? You just get hit all the time. You can't fight."

While a critical remark from their parent would discourage most kids, Roach took it up as a challenge and started practicing with extreme discipline to improve himself. He soon became so good that he started beating his elder brother in fights too.

The Epitome of Unmet Potential

Roach met the legendary coach Eddie Futch when he turned eighteen. During training, he perfected the hardest maneuvers Futch taught him. But during the heat of the moment in the ring, he would forget his training. His fights would often turn into brawls and he would often lose.

Roach was the epitome of potential not being met. When he lost five out of six matches, he quit. He took on a job as a telemarketer. But boxing still called him and he went to the gym where Futch trained just to see other boxers in action.

He soon started helping Futch train the fighters. He knew all of Futch's techniques very well and was a good coach himself.

Becoming an Exceptional Coach

One day, he picked up a lesson from the field of martial arts fighting. In boxing, one usually practices his maneuvers on a punching bag. But in martial arts fighting, the trainers wear large padded mitts that the fighters practice kicking on.

Roach quickly realized that padded mitts were superior to punching bags because they were not stationary. A trainer could wear them and enter the ring himself. Roach knew what was lacking from his training. There was no heat and pressure during practice. And so excellence in practice didn't transfer well to actual fights. But with padded mitts, Roach could enter in the ring and train the fighters dynamically. He could demonstrate strategic moves in real time. Training could now emulate real fights a lot closer.

With this new technique of training, Roach soon became an exceptional trainer even better than his teacher Futch. Over the years, he had trained twenty-seven boxers to become world champions!

Action Summary:

- Observe and learn from other industries.
- Make sure your training and education is as close to live action as possible. Be an apprentice, not a student.

THOMAS EDISON

Thomas Edison: The Worst Fisherman That Ever Lived

Thomas Alva Edison had been one of the most successful scientists the world had ever seen. He invented the phonograph, the motion picture, and the electric light bulb. In all, Edison had 1,093 U.S. patents under his name.

But people observed that as brilliant as Edison was at inventing new gadgets, he was just as miserable as a fisherman. Edison used to spend an hour almost every day sitting at the end of a dock and fish. He always fished all alone by himself, but he never caught any fish.

The Reason Behind Being a Lousy Fisherman

People always wondered: why was Edison so obsessed with fishing when he was so bad at it? Late in life, someone actually asked Edison as to the reason behind him being a lousy fisherman.

His answer was, "I really never caught any fish because I have never used any bait."

Thinking that Edison was crazy, a follow-up question was asked of him: "Why in the world would you fish without bait?"

Edison's answer: "Because when you fish without bait, people don't bother you and neither do the fish. It provides me my best time to think."

It's no coincidence that the world's best scientist was also the world's worst fisherman. In fact, because Edison was the world's worst fisherman, he could become the world's most prolific scientist. Edison realized early that, at rest, brain switches from information gathering mode to pattern recognizing mode which leads to a lot of breakthroughs.

Action Summary:

* Set some alone time aside for yourself to reflect and think on ideas.

Alexander Graham Bell

Alexander Graham Bell's Mistake That Leads to the Invention of the Telephone

Alexander Graham Bell was all of twelve years old when his mother started losing her hearing. So Bell learnt a manual finger language he could use to let his mother know about the conversations that occur in the family parlor. He later developed a way of speaking in clear tones directly into his mother's forehead so that she could hear him.

His mother's deafness led Bell to study acoustics. When Bell was sixteen years old, his father took him and his brothers to see a unique automaton created by Sir Charles Wheatstone. The mechanical machine simulated a human voice. Bell and his elder brother Melvin spent a lot of time learning everything they could about building an automaton. They then proceeded to build one that said the word "mama."

From Automatons to Dogs

After the automaton, Bell continued with his studies of acoustics with a live subject: their family dog. He would reach into the dog's mouth and manipulate the vocal cords to see how it changed the dog's voices.

Learning from the dog's vocal cords, Bell started experimenting on tuning forks to further explore the transmission of sound. At the age of nineteen, Bell wrote a report on his research which was read by Alexander Ellis—a friend of Bell's father. Alexander Ellis immediately pointed out that similar work was done by a German physicist named Hermann von Helmholtz. He procured the physicists book and sent it to Bell.

The German Mistranslations that Changed the World

Bell was quite dismayed to know that someone else had already done research on his ideas. But being curious, he ventured to read the physicists book. The book was however written in German. So Bell had to rely on translated works. And thankfully for the world, the translations were erroneous.

Hermann von Helmholtz had created a machine that used tuning forks and resonant chambers to recreate vowel sounds. Hermann was generating vowel sounds artificially, but because of the erroneous translation, Bell thought that Hermann was transmitting vowel sounds electrically over a wire. And the only reason his own research was trailing Hermann's was because of his lack of knowledge about electronics.

So Bell ventured forward to remedy that and started learning and experimenting with electromagnetism and sound. He figured that if vowels could be produced electrically by Harmann, then so could consonants, and so could entire speeches and conversations. And he tried to figure out ways on how that could be done.

And because of these experiments, he later on invented the telephone. But if Bell had known German, he would have never gone on to conduct his experiments with electricity and invented the telephone!

Action Summary:

- If you work hard enough, luck will assist you. Impossible is nothing.
- You can be beaten by tragedies. Or you can be challenged by them and try to find ways on how to improve your situation.
- Gradual buildup of your tackling your challenges is what will lead to immense success.

Steve Jobs

Steve Jobs Secret to Creating Revolutionary Products

Steve Jobs was not an easy person to work with, especially, when times were bad. When sales of the new Macintosh computer released in 1984 were poor, it led to a power struggle between Jobs and John Sculley—the Pepsi CEO Jobs had recruited to lead Apple.

Employees found Jobs to be too temperamental. He often called meetings at midnight and wrote lengthy faxes that amounted to nothing. Finally, in 1985, the Apple board fired Steve Jobs.

In a turn of events, Steve Jobs returned to Apple in 1996, when Apple bought his new company NeXT. He became the CEO of Apple again by 1997. Jobs had however learnt his lesson and had become better with people. He wasn't perfect and was still temperamental and dictatorial. But he was more likeable than before.

Getting Rid of the Product Line

The outside world did not see the change in Steve Jobs however. When Jobs decided to cut Apple products from 350 to 10, everyone derided him. He cut away things like the printer that everyone thought was essential for a computer company. The stock price dipped and people thought Jobs would run Apple to the ground.

But Jobs didn't allow that to change his mind. Instead of creating 350 crappy products, or even hundred good products, he decided to make ten awesome well-designed products.

And now that he didn't have to focus Apple's resources on 350 mediocre products, he could focus all his energy on the next big thing. Because he stopped manufacturing the printer in 1997, he could come out with the iPod in 2001 and change Apple's fortunes.

Action Summary:

- Focus. Do one thing really well instead of doing ten things just ok.
- As Steve Jobs says: "People think focus means saying yes to the thing you've got to focus on. But that's not what it means at all. It means saying no to the hundred other good ideas that there are. Innovation is saying 'no' to 1,000 things."

Jay Z

How Jay Z Leverages Small Successes to Become a Super Hit Rapper

Jay Z, whose real name was Shawn Carter, had a rough and poor childhood. He was the youngest of four siblings. His father abandoned the family when Jay Z was eleven years old. Jay Z lived in the projects in Brooklyn, New York with his mother and siblings.

He soon started dealing crack cocaine and dropped out of school. Violence was a part of his life and Jay Z was shot thrice during these days. But music saved him.

Jay Z started participating in various rap battles in his neighborhood. He soon became the hype man for Big Daddy Kane. His job was to increase the audience excitement with exclamations and interjections, and be a backup rapper for Big Daddy Kane.

Soon he started building a name for himself and wrote his own rap singles. But he failed to get a recording deal with any record label. Jay Z created his record label with two of his friends and started selling his records from his car!

Selling from His Car to Becoming a Star

After a year of doing this, he could show some numbers and could convince Priority Records to give him a shot, sign him up, and help distribute his album "Reasonable Doubt." Jay Z used another strategy to promote his album.

He got other rappers and DJs like the Notorious B.I.G and DJ Premier to collaborate on the album with him. And because of the collaborations, these musicians got on board to promote his album too. The album did relatively well and reached number twenty-three on the billboards!

Jay Z then rinsed and repeated his strategy. He leveraged his previous album's success and convinced Def Jam records to distribute his next album "In My Lifetime, Vol. 1." And he got some even more famous people like Foxy Brown, Lil' Kim and P. Diddy to collaborate on a few of the songs in the album.

And this time, Jay Z sold over a million copies of his new album—earning Platinum status!

Action Summary:

* Hustle. Do what you can with what you have—when others reject you.
* Leverage your small successes to get bigger and better deals.
* Collaborate with others and they will help promote you.

Demosthenes

How Demosthenes Becomes the Greatest Greek Orator Who Ever Lived

Demosthenes lived in ancient Athens in 384 BC. When he was sixteen years old, a great trial was going on in the courts of Athens. And Demosthenes went to see it. The court house was packed with over 1500 people. A lawyer named Callistratus was arguing the case. He spoke for four hours. And he was so good that not a single person left the courtroom!

Callistratus won the case with ease. And it made Demosthenes want to become a lawyer and a great orator too.

But Demosthenes was awful when he first begun. His first speech in the public assembly in Athens bombed. He stammered. His voice was uneven and not loud enough. His face convulsed the harder he tried. And on top of that, he suffered from rhotacism and had trouble pronouncing the letter "r" a lot of the times. People laughed at him. And even his friends said that he would never become a good orator.

Demosthenes' Public Speaking Plan

But Demosthenes didn't give up. He came up with a plan to break the elements of public speaking down and master each of them one at a time.

* To become better with his content and structure of the arguments, he copied and wrote down famous historical speeches 8–10 times by hand.
* To not be confused with the noise of the crowd at the assembly hall, and to make sure his voice would be heard, he went to the seashore and recited his speeches there amidst the roar of the waves.
* To enunciate the words better and not to stammer, he practiced his speeches by stuffing his mouth with stones.
* To have a better posture while speaking, and to overcome his poor habit of raising one shoulder over another, he suspended a sword so that it would prick him if he raised his shoulders.
* To coordinate his words with his breathing, he recited his speeches while running up the hill.
* To make sure he practiced diligently every day without diversion, he often shaved one side of his head. So that he would be forced to remain indoors and practice for a couple of months at a time.

With these efforts, Demosthenes became one of the greatest Greek orators who ever lived. People flocked to see him speak at the assembly. When Athens had to send someone to persuade another Greek state to become an ally, they would send Demosthenes. Because he delivered!

Action Summary:

- With enough practice and hard work, you can become better at anything.
- Break things done to its simplest elements and conquer each one of them one at a time.

Jay Leno

The Strategy Jay Leno Uses To Build His Audience

Jay Leno was one of the most successful comedians and TV anchors. He hosted the "Tonight Show with Jay Leno" from 1992 to 2009, and again from 2010 to 2014. And his show received higher ratings and viewers than other late night talk shows consistently year after year. For twenty-one straight years!

But no one thought Leno would be successful. His high school counselor actually recommended that Leno should drop out because he was dyslexic. But Leno decided that he just had to work a lot harder than others to get the same things.

Leno Becomes a Comedian

Leno knew from a very young age that he wanted to become a comedian. When he was studying in Emerson College, he actually started a local comedy club because none was available.

Critics hated Leno. But somehow the audience loved him. Leno put in more effort than other comedians in his routines. He worked very hard in refining his jokes and perfecting his delivery. And over time, he built his own unique style.

Leno's Trick to Pack the Room

After college, Leno hit the stand-up circuit. He went from town to town performing at various shady clubs. But he thought that he wasn't succeeding fast enough. People didn't know him and so many of his performances were in sparsely filled rooms.

Leno decided to do something about it. He started performing a free show for cab drivers and their spouses. He would hold special shows for cab drivers at 2:00 in the morning.

As a result, whenever someone asks the cabbie "What's happening in the city?" or "What's the best thing to do in the night?" the cab driver would tell them to go and see Jay Leno's comedy show.

And because of this one tactic, Leno soon found himself in rooms packed with people. His fame started growing which led to him getting invited on the Tonight Show with Johnny Carson and succeeding as the host of the show when Carson retired in 1992.

Action Summary:

- Work harder than others. Especially when things are stacked against you.
- Influence the influential. Give a free sample to the people who are in a position to drive others to you.

ELVIS PRESLEY

How Elvis Presley Makes More Money Dead Than Alive

The year was 1979 and Priscilla Presley—the wife of late Elvis Presley—was in shock. Vernon Presley, Elvis's father was the executor of his estate of $4.9 million after Elvis's death in 1977. But when Vernon himself passed away in 1979, Priscilla got the reigns in her hand. Under Elvis' will, the estate was to be held in a trust for his daughter Lisa Marie until she turned twenty-five in the year 1993.

But in 1979 when Priscilla became the executor, she found out that the estate won't last that long. It was bleeding money. Fast. Elvis had sold off 700 master recordings of his songs recorded before 1973 to RCA for a paltry sum, and the royalty coming in for all his post-1973 songs was about $500,000 a year and decreasing year after year. This was not enough to even pay for maintenance and insurance of Elvis's Memphis home in Graceland.

By 1981, the estate only had $560,000 in cash. And then the U.S. government recalculated the value of the estate and slapped a $10 million inheritance tax—even though the estate was losing money!

Surely, the estate would go bankrupt. Priscilla had to do something.

Voyeuristic Marketing: Creating a Legend

Instead of admitting defeat, cutting the losses, selling the Graceland property and paying off the government, Priscilla decided to make a legend out of a dead singer. She invested all of $560,000 back into the Graceland mansion, converted it into a museum, and opened it to the public in June of 1982.

The estate recouped its investment of $560,000 within thirty-eight days!

People clamored to visit the Graceland mansion and discover how Elvis lived!

By 1988 (eleven years after Elvis's death), dead Elvis was making more money than live Elvis ever had! And by 1999, 600,000 people visited Graceland every year, bringing in more than $20 million annually!

Action Summary:

* People are voyeuristic in nature. We are curious. And we want to find out what happens behind the scenes. Let people in on secrets and they will come to you in hordes!
* Letting people peek behind the scenes is the best way to let them know why you do what you do. It's the best way to showcase how awesome your stuff is.

Sam Walton

Sam Walton and His Strategy of Saturation

Sam Walton was the founder of Wal-Mart. If he were alive today, and his fortune not been divided between his wife and four kids, he would be worth more than twice the net worth of Bill Gates. He would be the richest person living—by a huge margin!

But when Sam started out, people didn't really think he would be successful. People from the retail industry didn't pay any attention to him at all. No one thought that opening superstores in towns with a population of less than 10,000 people would work.

Why would they? When the supermarket gold rush was going on in United States in the 1960s and the 1970s, companies like Kmart were doing their best to be the first company to open up their stores in the biggest metropolitan areas—as quickly as they could—while Sam took a completely contrarian approach. Instead of opening stores all over America, Sam started opening stores close to each other.

Focus and Saturate

Sam would focus on a particular region and then would hop on board an airplane. Up from the air, he would pin point locations close to each other where his Wal-Mart stores could come up.

This strategy of focusing and saturating a smaller region with his stores made Wal-Mart, a household name, in the area Sam focused on. When Kmart and other companies tried to enter these markets, they found it pretty hard to capture market share. It was almost impossible to compete against Wal-Mart in the regions it dominated.

Using this simple strategy of saturation, Wal-Mart took on behemoths like Kmart who had millions of dollars to spend and beat them.

Action Summary:

* Don't try to wear yourself thin. Focus and saturate. Pick a niche or an area and dominate it completely. Then pick a related niche or area.
* Don't choose to follow what everyone else is doing in the industry. Take a contrarian approach.

Marie Curie

How Marie Curie Became the Most Famous Female Scientist

Marie Curie was famous for being the first woman to win a Nobel Prize. She won not one, but two Nobel Prizes—in two different fields: Physics and Chemistry. The catalyst for her fame was her giving nature.

When Marie was a young girl in Poland, mainstream higher educational institutions did not allow women in. Just so that her elder sister could go to Paris and study medicine, Marie worked as a governess for over three years and provided financial help to her sister. Marie herself continued her education reading books and exchanging letters.

When an opportunity arose for Marie herself to go to Paris to study, she refused because she didn't have enough money. She spent a year and a half saving money before she could go to Paris herself.

Life in Paris

Even in Paris, her helpfulness was noticed by other folks, and, in return, they went out of their way to help Marie when she needed help. In fact, when one of her colleagues learnt that Marie was looking for lab space to conduct a few experiments, he put her in touch with Pierre Curie who was a professor at the School of Physics and Chemistry. They both fell in love and that's how Marie Sklodowska became Marie Curie.

In 1903, Marie Curie jointly won her first Nobel Prize because of her research in radiation. In 1911, she won her second Nobel for discovering the new elements of radium and polonium. But even though Marie was advancing the field of science by leaps and bounds, she didn't get the recognition she deserved from the French government.

The French Academy of Science didn't elect her as a member by one or two votes. A lot of people in power didn't like her because she was a foreigner and an atheist. And, as a result, Marie constantly had to hustle for better lab equipment and resources.

Only when Marie started receiving invitations from Poland to come and settle there, the French government decided to build the Radium Institute where world class equipment would be provided for further research in radioactivity.

Life During the War

The Radium Institute's development however was interrupted because of World War I. Marie put her heart and soul in helping the soldiers during the war. She went from hospital to hospital helping them set up radiology labs and X-ray machines.

She spent time learning automotive mechanics so that she could build mobile radiography units that could be used at the front lines.

When radium was in low supply, she provided one gram of it—worth over $100,000—from her own stash. (Over 1.2 million dollars in 2014)

It was estimated that over a million wounded soldiers were treated by one of her X-ray units!

But Marie Curie was never given recognition for her war effort from the French government. And no help was provided to her when she was struggling to find more radium to continue her research either.

Becoming World Famous

When Missy Meloney—a journalist—was in Paris, she went to interview Marie. She was so outraged to hear about her struggles to find more radium that she set up a Marie Curie Radium Fund. She enlisted the help of other journalists back in United States to help her promote the fund and persuaded Marie Curie to come tour the United States.

Because of these efforts, Marie Curie's fame grew! She was no longer someone only the scientists knew—she became a household name!

The President of United States, Warren Harding, himself agreed to present a gift of one gram of radium to Marie Curie. The day before Marie was to meet Warren Harding, however, she came to know that the radium was going to be gifted to her personally. She complained. The radium should be gifted to science, not to her. She made them call in a lawyer at the last moment so that the radium could be gifted to her lab instead to her personally.

Over her entire life, even though Marie Curie faced a lot of setbacks, she never let it sour her. She kept on living her life not for herself but for others.

Action Summary:

- Be helpful. Help with no expectations in return. Things will work out.

* No one has achieved anything of importance without struggle. The more stories people hear about your struggles, the more fame you will get.

Jeff Bezos

Jeff Bezos and the Two-Pizza Rule

Jeff Bezos started Amazon.com in 1994. He quit his cushy job in the field of finance and moved from New York to Seattle to start Amazon because he saw huge potential in the Internet.

Amazon started out with books but steadily increased their categories and started selling everything from toys to kitchenware to clothes. As Amazon grew, so did the levels of management the company had, and along with that the bureaucracy in the company.

So as most big companies did, Bezos organized an offsite retreat for all the managers and executives at Amazon. At the retreat, folks started brainstorming on how to grow Amazon and solve the various problems it faced.

One manager got up and said that employees should start communicating with each other a lot more to build consensus. Bezos vehemently disagreed and declared: "No! Communication is terrible."

Communication is Terrible

Bezos knew that building consensus would lead to groupthink. It would kill off a lot of ideas and innovation because good ideas come from opposing views. He wanted independent ideas to pop up from anywhere in the company. He wanted people to not be scared to come forth with their ideas and opinions—even if it was not a popular one.

And so Bezos came up with a company-wide rule—The two-pizza rule. No team should be big enough that it couldn't be fed with two pizzas. He said, "Let's have small independent teams where people put in more effort into their work and less effort into communication and building consensus."

Different Views Lead to Awesomeness

Bezos also allowed buyers to post negative reviews for the products they had purchased. When he started allowing negative reviews, everyone told him that it was a dumb decision. That negative reviews would reduce sales. Why would an ecommerce website do something that would reduce their sales? But Bezos proved everybody wrong. Because what negative reviews did was reduced the sales of bad products but increased the trust in the overall company and increased overall sales.

When Amazon bought Zappos for 1.2 billion dollars in 2009—Bezos did not try to integrate Zappos into Amazon. He gave them complete autonomy. He allowed them to retain their own company culture and procedures because Bezos knew that different views and opinions would lead to awesomeness rising up.

Action Summary:

* Fight groupthink. Disagreements are not always bad because it leads to better ideas and innovation.
* Work in small teams so that you can have the best of both worlds. Less bureaucracy along with less groupthink. Implement the two-pizza rule!

ALFRED NOBEL

Alfred Nobel Creates His Legacy

Alfred Nobel is known for the Nobel Prize awards that are given out every year to recognize excellence in the fields of physics, chemistry, physiology or medicine, literature, and peace. During his lifetime, Nobel earned 355 patents and was a brilliant engineer. He earned his first patent when he was only twenty-four years old. He was the inventor of dynamite. Alfred Nobel was a genius.

As a young boy, Nobel excelled in chemistry and languages. He spoke five languages fluently: Swedish, English, French, German, and Russian. When Nobel was seventeen years old, he went to Paris to further study chemistry. And a year later when he turned eighteen, he went to United States to study chemistry for four more years.

Dynamites and Detonators

After studies, Nobel joined the family business of manufacturing armaments. While his elder brother Ludvig ran the business, Nobel devoted himself to the study of explosives—especially how to manufacture and use nitroglycerine safely—which was extremely unstable. He invented the detonator that allowed triggering an explosive device at a distance. And he also designed the blasting cap that makes transportation of explosives from one place to another a lot safer.

In 1864, a shed used for preparation of nitroglycerine exploded killing five people including Nobel's younger brother Emil. This affected Nobel greatly and he doubled down on developing safer explosives. In 1867, he invented dynamite which was a lot more stable than nitroglycerine. Mining and construction of industries became a lot safer because of dynamite.

Before his death in 1896, Nobel built ninety armaments factories in various parts of Europe and America. And along with his business empire, his investments in the Caspian oil fields made him one of the richest people in the nineteenth century. But when one invests in guns and oil, his reputation suffers.

The Merchant of Death is Dead

In 1888, Nobel's elder brother Ludvig passed away. But a French paper made a mistake and published Alfred's obituary instead of his brother's. The title of the article was "The merchant of death is dead." The article was very unflattering and started off with "Dr. Alfred Nobel, who became rich by finding ways to kill more people faster than ever before, died yesterday."

This affected Nobel deeply. It made him think about what kind of a legacy he wanted to leave behind. How he wanted to be remembered.

And so without telling anyone, Alfred Nobel formed a new will in which he bequeathed 94% of his wealth—31,225,000 Swedish Kronor—to start a fund to establish the five Nobel Prizes!

Today, Alfred Nobel is remembered not as the merchant of death, but as the patron of science and literature; as the kindler of peace.

Action Summary:

* Reward people and you will be remembered fondly.
* You don't have to wait till you die to start rewarding people. And you don't have to reward people with money either. Sincere praise is reward enough. Encourage people with your words.

Bill Gates

Bill Gates and the Start of Microsoft

Nineteen-year-old Bill Gates had an epiphany while reading the January 1975 issue of Popular Electronics. Altair 8800—a microcomputer—was featured on the cover of the magazine. It was one of the first computers that could fit on a desk. The computers that came before Altair 8800 took up whole rooms.

Altair 8800 was being sold by mail order through advertisements in various hobby magazines and journals. And while the designers had expected to sell only a few hundred units, they ended up collecting a few thousand orders in the first month itself.

Gates realized that the computers would keep on becoming smaller and cheaper. Demand for it would only go up and up. Selling software for these computers could become a viable business.

So Bill Gates joined forces with his friend Paul Allen and started Microsoft—a company that would make and sell software for the microcomputers.

Microsoft's First Product

Their first order of business: they contacted Ed Roberts—the maker of Altair 8800—and told him that they were developing an interpreter for the BASIC computing language that would work on Altair 8800. They asked whether he would be interested in seeing a demo.

BASIC allowed people other than mathematicians and scientists to create code and run it on computers. A BASIC interpreter would allow business men and hobbyists to use their computer. So Roberts agreed to meet them for a demo in a few days' time.

At this point of time, however, Gates and Allen had not created the BASIC interpreter. Gates did not want to spend time making something before he knew he would be able to sell it. Once they found that the idea had demand, they put in the effort to bring it to life.

The next hurdle was that being students, Gates and Allen didn't have the money to buy an Altair 8800 to build their interpreter for it.

But Paul Allen had created an emulator for a time sharing computer before. He modified and adapted it after reading the Altair programmer guide and tested it on a different machine—on one of Harvard's time sharing computers without permission.

On the day of the demo, Paul Allen flew down to Albuquerque to meet with Roberts. And only when the BASIC interpreter opened up on Altair 8800 successfully, he knew that the code worked on the hardware.

Repeating the Trick with IBM

In 1980, IBM was working on the IBM PC. Microsoft contacted them to sell Microsoft BASIC for IBM computers. During the negotiations, Bill Gates and Paul Allen found that IBM was having a hard time licensing the operating system for their computers. Digital Research—a company that was the leader of operating systems at the time—was not agreeing to a deal.

Bill Gates asked them whether IBM would license their operating system if they developed it. On getting an affirmative answer, they started looking for a solution.

They quickly approached the Seattle Computer Products company that had built this operating system called QDOS: quick and dirty operating system. They signed an agreement where Microsoft would pay them $10,000 upfront and a royalty for every company they sold the operating system to. The name of QDOS was changed to MS-DOS.

The MS-DOS Deal

Bill Gates then went back to IBM and negotiated a deal to license MS-DOS for $45,000. On the negotiation table, IBM thought that they had got the best out of Microsoft because they expected to pay a lot more for the operating system. Bill Gates and Microsoft didn't even ask for a royalty per computer sale.

But Bill Gates knew what he was doing. In exchange for keeping the price low, Bill Gates wanted the ability to sell MS-DOS to other companies too. He realized that the computer market would grow bigger than any one company could handle. He wanted a piece of all of it instead of being tied down to one company alone.

And by not charging a royalty per sale, Bill Gates made sure that IBM pushed MS-DOS the hardest. When Digital Research finally came onboard to license their operating system CP/M, IBM priced MS-DOS for $40 while pricing CP/M at $240.

In 1981, Microsoft bought complete rights to QDOS for $50,000 to avoid paying any royalties. And MS-DOS soon became the default operating system which enabled Microsoft to build an empire on top of it!

Action Summary:

- Start building only after you're certain that there is demand for your product.
- Don't base your negotiation on price alone. Think of how you can capture a huge market share.
- Keep an eye out for trends in your industry.

Chanakya

Chanakya Unites India

About 2400 years ago, there was no India. The Indian subcontinent was divided into various princely states and independent kingdoms. Chanakya was a teacher and a scholar who lived in the city of Takshashila during this era. He was known to be the smartest person alive, and had mastered economics, political science, warfare, mathematics, medicine, and various religious texts.

In 326 BC, Alexander the Great attacked and defeated Porus and his kingdom of Paurava in North-West India. This defeat led to a lot of refugees migrating to Takshashila.

Chanakya realized that if Porus would have joined hands with other neighboring kingdoms, Alexander may not have won the battle. India needs to be united and made strong or else it would only be a matter of time before other foreign rulers conquered India.

So Chanakya went to Pataliputra—the biggest and the strongest kingdom of that time—in an attempt to help the Nanda King who ruled the city to unite India. But the Nanda King took one look at Chanakya, saw how ugly he was, and threw him out.

Then and there Chanakya took an oath: he would defeat the Nanda King and unite India.

Chanakya Finds his King

Chanakya needed to find a king. So he went and visited other kingdoms and princely states and vetted a few other kings and princes but found them either weak or unambitious or petty to lead the effort to unite India.

While pondering whom he should back in the quest to unite India, Chanakya realized that he was doing things backwards. He was searching for a prince who may have kingly qualities. Instead he should search for the quality that makes someone a good king, and then guide the person who has that quality to become the king.

As soon as Chanakya had this epiphany, he realized that he already knew the perfect candidate to become the king. One of the young boys that he taught already had the quality all good kings need. Whenever a fight erupted amongst the kids, the kids went to the sixteen-year-old Chandragupta Maurya and asked him to judge and decide who was at fault. And Chandragupta Maurya's decisions were always just. Chanakya knew that justice was the one quality a king needs above all else. And so he decided to back Chandragupta Maurya.

Chanakya had his king. But he didn't have his army yet. So he approached a few kings in the hilly regions neighboring the Nanda Empire—knowing that they didn't like Nanda King—and convinced them to lend a small part of their army to his efforts to beat the Nanda King. He then trained Chandragupta to go from village to village and give uproarious speeches that would incite the villagers to join and grow the army. With both these efforts, he built an army that was almost as big as that of his foe.

Chanakya Defeats the Nanda King

Chanakya and Chandragupta Maurya challenged the Nanda King to a war. But they found that Nanda King had a better trained army guided by a war strategist who was as good as Chanakya. And they failed to seize control. Both sides proved equal in a few small battles and they found themselves locked in a stalemate.

One time, while Chanakya was going from one base to another, he sat outside a small hut to rest for a minute. Inside the hut, he observed a child who was trying to eat khichdi—a hot rice dish. The child kept on burning his hand. So the mother scolded him to eat from the edges and not the center, as the center would always be hotter.

The moment leaded to a huge epiphany. Chanakya instantly sent a message to Chandragupta to retreat. He said not to fight any battles with the Nanda King directly, but instead to start conquering the small towns and villages at the edges of the Nanda Empire.

After a year of such small conquests at the edges, Chandragupta again challenged Nanda King directly. But this time he found that his army was bigger and that his soldiers were a bit more skillful, and so this time he won!

Chanakya and Chandragupta went on to unite the whole of India for the first time shortly after.

Action Summary:

* Go from the periphery to the center. Instead of jumping right into the center of a big problem, deal with it from the edges and make your way to the center.

* When your competition is huge, niche. And dominate one niche at a time until you become as big as your competitor.
* Team up with people based on merit.

Marco Polo

Marco Polo's Secret to Fame

No one had done more than Marco Polo to help the European powers grow. Marco Polo traveled to Asia from Venice when he was just seventeen years old and he spent the next twenty-four years of his life trading and living in Asia. He visited Persia, China, Indonesia, Burma, Tibet and India over his epic adventure.

Marco Polo's travel stories had inspired thousands of people. Christopher Columbus—the sailor who discovered America—was one such person who read Marco Polo's travel chronicles in his youth and was deeply inspired by it and wanted to visit those lands himself.

But most importantly, Marco Polo's travels inspired a lot of cartographers and map makers. Marco Polo had bought a map back to Venice from China. This map influenced the development of the European cartography movement. This ultimately led to undertaking of several European voyages of exploration over the next couple of centuries.

Marco Polo's Legacy

The Portuguese expeditions to Asia and Africa, as well as the Spanish voyages that led to the discovery and settlement of America, all of them were influenced by Marco Polo's stories.

But you know what? Marco Polo was not the first European to travel to Asia. Not by a long shot. There were hundreds of other merchants who had traveled to Asia before him. Amongst them were Marco Polo's father and uncle who actually took Marco Polo with them during their second trip to Asia.

But no one remembered the names of any of these other merchants and travelers. Why was Marco Polo so famous when others were forgotten?

Because Marco Polo chronicled his journey—He maintained a journal and wrote things down. This had made him the most famous traveler the world had ever known.

Action Summary:

* Chronicle your adventures. Write them down.
* Write and teach to become famous.

Napoleon Bonaparte

Napoleon Bonaparte's Secret to Earning Loyalty

Napoleon Bonaparte was one of the best tacticians the world had ever seen. He was the master of building alliances. When faced with two powers joining forces against him, he could maneuver in a way to break them apart and beat them one after the other.

But the Russian invasion dealt a big blow to Napoleon. Whenever Napoleon marched to engage the Russian army to a battle, the Russians would retreat deeper into Russia, giving away ground. But they would retreat after scorching the earth and leaving nothing behind that would allow Napoleon's army to sustain themselves.

But Napoleon still marched on because of his thirst to expand his empire. Napoleon lost more soldiers chasing the Russians than in any war he had waged and won before. He had started the Russian invasion with 400,000 soldiers and ended it with 40,000.

This weakened Napoleon's power considerably. Austria, Sweden, Russia, Great Britain, Spain, and Portugal saw an opportunity and formed a coalition and were finally able to exile Napoleon to the island of Elba and put up King Louis XVIII to rule France.

Escape from Exile

After about ten months staying in exile, Napoleon finally escaped. King Louis XVIII sent an entire regiment to intercept and capture Napoleon. When this regiment came face to face with Napoleon, Napoleon got down off his horse and shouted: "Here I am. Kill your emperor if you wish."

But instead of killing or capturing Napoleon, the soldiers responded with "Long Live the emperor" and marched with him to conquer Paris!

The Secret to Loyalty

Napoleon's ability to arouse loyalty was unmatched. How did Napoleon earn this loyalty even after losing badly? Yes, he was a good tactician and a good leader. Yes, he was charismatic. But Napoleon had one secret weapon.

He Gave away Baubles

Baubles were small ornaments that had little monetary value. But they had great emotional value attached to them. Napoleon gave baubles to his soldiers when they achieved a notable feat.

This recognition he gave to his best soldiers earned him their life-long loyalty. The tactic achieved two things:

1. Made his soldiers fight harder to earn more baubles.
2. Made his soldiers loyal to him.

The loyalty Napoleon earned was so strong that when he was finally beaten by the Duke of Wellington and exiled to Saint Helena in Africa, there were multiple attempts to rescue him every year. But because Saint Helena was an island in the middle of nowhere, and the closest mass of land was 1,800 kilometers away, no attempt succeeded.

Action Summary:

* Give away rewards. Recognize people for the good they do.
* Cut your losses early. Avoid pyrrhic victories that come with devastating costs.

Wilbur and Orville Wright

The Wright Brothers Build a Heavier Than Air Flying Machine

The year was 1881. Alexander Graham Bell invested a lot of his telephone money into building heavier than air flying machines. At almost the same time, the Smithsonian Institute funded the efforts of Professor Langley to create flying machines.

Over the next few years, a lot of other resourceful people with extensive backing got into the race of being the first ones to build an airplane. Millions of dollars were spent. But no one really succeeded.

Wilbur and Orville Wright were two brothers who owned a bicycle repair shop. They entered the airplane race eight years late—in 1889. They did not have a lot of money and weren't as resourceful as some of their competitors. But yet four years later, they were the first ones to build and successfully fly a heavier than air machine.

So how did the Wright brothers succeed where others more powerful and resourceful had failed?

Lesson from Bicycles

While others focused on creating more powerful engines, the Wright brothers took a different approach. They focused on creating a better shaped plane that provided better control and balance.

Their work with bicycles taught the Wright brothers that an unstable vehicle required better balance, and not more power. So they spent time and tested 200 types of wings and propellers. They perfected their glider and put in an engine much later—almost as an afterthought.

On so, on December 17, 1903, the Wright brothers were the first ones in the world to successfully fly a heavier than air machine. Their first flight lasted all of twelve seconds. But history was made.

Action Summary:

- Form before power. Smartness always beats brute force.
- Improve your services before improving your advertising.
- Don't give up even if you have competitors who are more resourceful than you. You can beat them by being more efficient than them.

Bonus: Aviation Biographies

Here is a special bonus prepared for you: a short report filled with genius biographies from the field of aviation:

- How the Chinese military strategist Zhuge Liang scares his opponents with the first use of a flying machine recorded in history?
- Was Leonardo Da Vinci the real inventor of flying machines?
- The simple tool Boeing uses to eliminate plane crashes
- The story of a statistician who saves the lives of hundreds of aircraft pilots during WW2

and more...

Go grab your copy:

http://geniusbiographies.com/aviation/

Tom Monaghan

Tom Monaghan Builds Domino's into World's Biggest Pizza Chain

Tom Monaghan was four years old when his father passed away. His mother was poor and couldn't manage to make ends meet, and so two years later, she placed Tom along with his brother James in an orphanage.

Tom's world view was influenced a lot by the nuns in the orphanage. And he decided to become a priest when he grew older. Unfortunately, he didn't have the discipline to lead the life of a priest and was expelled from the seminary. But Tom had the mindset of a fixer.

To fix his discipline problem, he joined the U.S. Marines and served them from 1956 to 1959. After his service, he joined the University of Michigan to study architecture. To pay for his education, Tom started searching for money-making opportunities.

The Start of Domino's

In 1960, he came across two brothers: Nick and Dominic who wanted to sell their pizza parlor named DomiNick's. Being in college, Tom knew that pizzas were something he could sell to students. So along with his brother James, Tom borrowed $500 and bought the pizza parlor and he renamed it to Domino's Pizza.

Unfortunately, Domino's Pizza was a loss-making business. Tom's brother James lost the heart to run it after a few loss-making months. But Tom had confidence in his abilities to turn things around. And so he bought his brothers stake by selling him his second hand car—his Volkswagen Beetle.

Tom knew that if he could turn his life around with discipline, he could turn the life of a pizza place around too. But things were tough. The architecture degree was put aside and Tom worked 100-hour weeks for the next thirteen years! The only vacation he took in this time was a six-day honeymoon right after his marriage.

Always a fixer, Tom invented the insulated pizza boxes that kept the pizzas warm during delivery and allowed multiple boxes to be stacked on top of another without squishing the pizzas inside—thus allowing more pizzas to be delivered in one trip.

But the real breakthrough for Domino's came during one of its worst days.

Hard Day Teaches a Big Lesson

One day, Tom found himself extremely understaffed. A lot of his employees could not make it to work on the same day for various different reasons. Tom knew that he would have to make some hard decisions or else he would not be able to cater to his patrons.

So he made a decision to cut off serving the six-inch pizza for the day to save time. The six-inch pizzas were the most popular dish ordered, and Tom thought that if he cut that out, maybe he would be able to cope with other orders.

But something surprising happened. While the total number of orders did go slightly down that day, the profits were up by 50%! It took the same amount of time to prepare the six-inch pizza as it took to prepare the eight-inch and ten-inch ones. When people could not buy the six-inch pizzas, they bought the bigger ones and Domino's earned more.

Simplifying the Menu

Tom realized that focus was the key. And he took things to their logical extreme. He immediately simplified his menu. He dropped sandwiches, other dishes and small-sized pizzas from it. Business began to boom.

What's more, his store's efficiency increased and he could now prepare and deliver orders quicker than his competitors. Tom created the now famous goal for himself: to deliver pizza fresh and hot within thirty minutes of the order.

This efficiency allowed him to expand and open more pizza outlets. But unlike other chains, Tom did not focus on opening his outlets in big cities. Instead, he focused on opening near college towns and military basis. Because he knew that focusing on towns that had a higher proportion of people ordering home delivery would lead to faster growth.

By 1980, Domino's had opened 200 stores! And things didn't slow down for the next two decades. There were days when three new Domino's opened per day. By 1998, there were 6,250 stores and Domino's had become the biggest pizza chain in the world!

Action Summary:

- Focus. Cut down on things. Simplification leads to greater efficiency which allows you to do things quicker than others.
- Back yourself. Believe in your abilities. Don't shy away from hard work and a tough journey ahead.

PT Barnum

How PT Barnum Hires a Beggar to Fill His Museum with People

Phineas Taylor Barnum was known as the greatest showman, the world had ever seen. He started his career by publishing a newsletter, but soon he moved to showmanship. He built the first aquarium in United States. His circus was the most popular circus in his era.

In 1841, thirty-one-year-old Barnum bought Scudder's American Museum in New York and renamed it to Barnum's American Museum.

Barnum's idea was not to own a boring museum that showed historically accurate artifacts. He wanted to wow people. Get them to talk about his museum. And so, he converted his museum into a combination of a zoo, a museum, a theatre, a freak show, a wax museum and a lecture hall.

He showcases everything from General Grant's hat to a "Feejee mermaid" to the trunk of a tree under which Jesus's disciples sat to beluga whales. He also held performances from magicians and ventriloquists and also organized prettiest baby contests.

Sending a Beggar on a Merry Go Round

One day, a plump beggar asked Barnum for a handout. Instead of paying him, Barnum offered him a job for one and a half dollars a day. He gave the beggar five bricks, and told him to place four bricks on the four street corners around the museum. Then walk to the first brick and replace it with the fifth brick. Then walk to the second brick and replace it with the first brick. Then walk to the third brick and replace it with the second brick. And so on for an entire hour.

At the end of the hour, the beggar had to show a ticket at the museum door and visit each and every room in the museum. Then leave and continue his brick replacement task. At no time was the beggar to converse with anyone and say what he was doing when asked.

Within the first hour, close to a thousand people started following the beggar to see what he was up to. When he entered the museum, a few dozen bought a ticket and entered behind him too. The beggar continued his brick replacement rigmarole for quite a few days. And every time he entered the museum, people followed him.

Barnum knew that it was not enough to have a really awesome showcase once people were inside his museums' doors. It was important to hook them beforehand with something out of the ordinary.

Action Summary:

- Do things that no one has done before. The trick to drawing crowds and getting people to talk about you is to do something that no one else has done before.
- Focus as much time in promoting your work as you do in producing it.
- Wow people. Always leave them with an amazing experience.

Benjamin Franklin

Benjamin Franklin Uses Psychology to Make Life-Long Friends

Benjamin Franklin was born in a busy household. He had nine brothers and sisters, and seven half brothers and sisters. Since he was one of seventeen siblings, he had to fight for attention. Because of this crowded upbringing, Franklin developed a keen sense of people early on. He learnt the art of persuasion and charming people's pants off.

Franklin the Book Lover

When Franklin was twelve years old, he apprenticed at the printing press his elder brother James ran. Here, Franklin got to read books and pamphlets on various topics. And he fell in love with reading and acquiring knowledge.

But books in the eighteenth century were expensive to own and hard to come by. So when Franklin turned twenty-one years old, he started a group called Junto. Franklin handpicked twelve people from diverse occupations and backgrounds and invited them to join the group—people whom he knew liked improving themselves while being helpful to others at the same time.

The members of Junto would share books with each other and meet once a week to discuss and debate on various topics and help each other network and make more money. Even though Franklin was the youngest of the group, he was undoubtedly the leader.

Franklin became the master of information gathering by reading on various topics and associating with people from diverse fields. This helped him a lot when he joined politics.

Franklin the Politician

Franklin easily won the elections for a clerk in the Pennsylvania general assembly when he was just thirty years old. But after a few years when he stood for his second term, he faced a tough fight from a rich and intelligent opponent.

Franklin wrote in his autobiography that the opponent gave a long speech that tarnished Franklin's reputation (Franklin doesn't name the opponent). Franklin won the reelection but he knew that he would have to win the opponent over too, because one day he might come to hold great power in the government.

Franklin Wins Over an Opponent

If one had to make an opponent their friend, one would usually try flattery. Maybe send a few gifts and go out of their way to be helpful. But Franklin knew a bit of human nature. And so he chose a completely opposite strategy to make his opponent like him.

Instead of doing the opponent a favor, Franklin asked the opponent to do him a favor. Franklin sent his rival a note asking to borrow a rare book for a week. The rival, feeling flattered, sent the book immediately. After reading the book, Franklin sent it back with a thank you note. The next time when the legislature opened, the rival approached Franklin and spoke to him at length for the first time. Franklin and his rival soon became friends. And this friendship lasted till his rival died years later!

Action Summary:

* Read a lot. Make friends from various fields. Become the information hub. And you will prosper.
* Human psychology is such that when you do someone a favor, you feel closer to them. If you know someone who doesn't like you much, ask them for a small favor—something they cannot say no to. Just the act of helping you out will make them like you.

Akio Morita

How Akio Morita Hires the Right People to Make Sony into a Huge Behemoth

Akio Morita was a lieutenant in the Japanese navy during World War II. After the war was over, he went to meet his friend Masaru Ibuka who was starting his own research lab. Both of them decided to start a company together where Ibuka would look after engineering and Akio Morita would bring in the money and look after marketing. They called their company "Tokyo Telecommunications Engineering Corporation" and it is one of the biggest companies in the world today. The company name was changed in 1958 and you may know it by that name. Sony.

World War II had ravaged Japan. A lot of good engineers who were soldiers in the war found themselves unemployed after the war was over. Akio Morita started hiring them even though, at that time, Sony was not doing very well and only sold a rice cooker. Akio Morita's savings were depleting at a fast rate but yet he gave a job to engineers who wanted one.

And that's because Akio Morita held the belief that gold can't always buy good soldiers. But good soldiers can always find gold. And he was proven right. Because while Sony stayed alive those initial months by repairing old radios and selling adaptors, its team of smart hardworking engineers soon started making world class products.

Sony was the company to sell the first tape recorder in Japan. And they received rave reviews.

But amongst the reviewers was also one persistent complainer.

Dealing with a Persistent Complainer

Norio was a music student and he found the quality of the tape recorder lacking. The tape recorders worked perfectly when it dealt with speech and conversations. But the voice wasn't as crisp with music—especially with transient sounds like those made by the piano. And so Norio would come and complain about it all the time. But unlike most complainers, Norio would also recommend tweaks and things that could be tried to make the sound better.

One day, Norio found himself arguing with Akio Morita himself. But instead of dismissing him, Morita was fascinated by him. Here was a musician who had interest in mechanics too. And he didn't act differently while complaining to the boss, he didn't sugarcoat things. Morita liked the brash honesty and so he asked Norio if he would like to come and work for Sony. Norio refused however because his dream was to be a musician.

Nurturing the Complainer

When Norio went to Germany to further his studies in music, Akio Morita asked him to keep in touch and send updates about the development of electronics in Europe. Morita also sent him a transistor radio when Sony developed it.

And a few years later, when Morita was going to Europe to find new agents for the transistor radio, he invited Norio to come along and help him. Throughout the trip, Morita goaded Norio to be frank and discuss what he thought was wrong with Sony.

And during the voyage back to Japan, when they were stuck in a ship for four days, Morita sprang his trap. After a fairly long discussion on what all Sony was doing poorly, Morita asked Norio: "Alright, why don't you come to Sony as a manager and fix it?"

After a little bit more persuasion, Norio agreed. And he became a rising star in Sony. It was Norio Ohga who led the development of the compact discs. And it was the same complaining Norio Ohga who succeeded as the chairman of Sony after Akio Morita.

Action Summary:

- Gold can't always buy good soldiers. But good soldiers can always find gold. Do everything you can to work with smart capable people.
- Don't shun away from complaints. See what you can learn from them.
- When you see someone talented, put in the effort to nurture them.

Princess Diana

Princess Diana's Becomes the People's Princess

Diana Spencer was born in a home longing for a boy. Her parents John and Frances Spencer were British aristocrats and wanted a male heir to carry on their family name. But their first child was a daughter and so was their second child. Their third child was a son—but he sadly passed away within ten hours of being born and their fourth child was again a daughter: Diana.

Diana was a disappointment to her parents. They didn't even name her for a week after birth, because they wanted a son. Their fifth child thankfully was a son. But it was brutal for Diana as she was the ignored child. As a result, she became a very shy kid.

The Fairytale Romance

When Diana was sixteen years old, she met Prince Charles because he was dating her elder sister Sarah. A few years later, when Prince Charles was thirty-one years old and had not yet married and produced a heir, a list was drawn up for him with suitable candidates for marriage. Nineteen-year-old Diana Spencer was short listed.

Diana got her fairytale romance when a prince courted her. But it was hard for a shy kid to be thrown in the public limelight. More than 750 million people witnessed her wedding on TV on July 29, 1981. And each and every one of those observers could make out that she was inexperienced and introverted—even through TV!

Princess Diana gave birth to two sons in short order. But after that, her marriage was not a happy one and was fraught with infidelities on both sides. And in 1992, the royal couple separated.

In 1997, a tragic car crash ended Diana's life at the young age of thirty-six. But by the time of her death, the shy and dorky girl had somehow transformed herself into being the most charismatic and loved personality of the world. Her fame and popularity surpassed that of the Queen. And more people cried on her death than anyone else's in the history of the world.

The Princess Transformation

How did a young and shy princess turn herself into one of the most charismatic and loved personality of the world?

To let you in on a secret, she was still shy. But she made an effort to reach out to people which gave her an image of being charismatic.

Her big secret? She wrote thank you letters to everyone from waiters and servers to security guards and drivers to CEOs and presidents. Everyone from top to bottom received a thank you note from the princess and then became her personal evangelists.

She transformed herself from a dull and dorky kid to the charismatic and kind princess—not by changing herself, but by thanking people around her and thus changing their perception of her.

Action Summary:

* Thank people. Sincerely praising people is the most effective way in getting them to like you.
* Be like a farmer who sows seeds everywhere. Thank everyone—big and small.

MICHAEL DELL

Young Michael Dell's Entrepreneurial Adventures

Michael Dell had always been a go-getter. When he was twelve years old, he started collecting stamps. He was fascinated about how people make money buying and selling stamps.

When he heard about a stamp auction being held nearby, he joined a Chinese restaurant as a dishwasher to earn some money—to buy some stamps at the auction. Michael then made a catalog of stamps, he and his friends own, and sold them directly via mail order without any middle man. He earned a cool $2,000 for this endeavor!

Michael Sells Newspapers

A few years later, when Michael was in high school, he wanted to buy a car for himself. He got a job at Houston Post to sell newspaper subscriptions. He was given a random list of people every week who didn't subscribe the newsletter. He had to go to them and persuade them to subscribe. It was a numbers game.

Michael made a few sales but nothing to boast about. But as he made more sales, he started seeing a pattern. There were two types of people who were more prone to buy a newspaper subscription than anyone else:

1. People who had just moved to a new house
2. And people who had just married

Once Michael discovered this pattern, he started thinking about how he could reach these people as soon as they had moved or married. He asked a few people for ideas and received a great one: go to the local court house and go through the records.

He threw away the list of random people he received from Houston Post, and started compiling his own list from the court house records. He went through each and every person who applied for a marriage license or filed a new mortgage application. And his sales shoot up. He soon hired a couple of friends to go and collect these records from court houses while he spent all his time selling.

Within one year of working part time at Houston Post, Michael earned $18,000. That was more than the salary his teachers make. He bought a brand new BMW for himself at the end of the year.

Michael Sells Computers

Later on, when Michael started his computer assembling business from his dorm room, these were the lessons that he implemented again to grow:

1. He created a list of people who would most need computers in bulk: government institutions, universities, and growing businesses.
2. He cut out the middle man to keep his costs low, and started selling computers directly to people who need it. Because his cost was lower than others, he started winning a lot of contracts from government as well as big corporates.

Because of these two strategies, Michael did business of about six million dollars in his first year of setting shop! His company: Dell ends up becoming the biggest computer seller in the world!

Action Summary:

* Track patterns. Figure out what is common between your best clients. And develop a marketing plan accordingly.
* Focus all your efforts in pin pointing and selling to people who are most willing and able to buy your wares.
* Don't bloat your expenses. Keep your costs low and you can outsell your competitors by offering lower prices.

Kobe Bryant

Kobe Bryant Builds on His Talent

Kobe Bryant was gifted. Everyone could see that he had talent. Even his father Joe Bryant—who was himself a retired basketball player—could see that Kobe was more talented than him and would go places.

Kobe Bryant started dominating the basketball court from a very young age. He was so talented that his high school basketball games attracted ticket scalpers!

The Decision to Skip College

But no one was happy when Bryant decided to skip college and go directly to the NBA. Bryant was only the sixth player in the entire NBA history to skip college and apply for the NBA draft right after high school.

People thought that he was cocky and chasing fame. What would he do if he failed in NBA? But Bryant knew his life goal. It was to become the best basketball player out there. And college would not help him with that.

He knew that he could become better faster if he played with better players. The practice and coaching he received while playing for a NBA team would be a lot better than any college could provide.

Why Talent Alone is Not Enough

Bryant also knew that talent alone would not make him the world's best player. There were others in the NBA league, who were more talented and experienced than him. To become better than them, Bryant would have to put in the hours to practice. So Bryant decided that he would work harder and put in more hours than all the other basketball players.

Bryant's normal day started earlier than other athletes. He would start his conditioning work at around 4:30 am. After an hour or so, he would work on strength training exercises for about forty-five minutes.

From 7:00 am to 11:00 am, he would practice alone on a skill he wanted to improve. It was not unusual to see him make 800 jump shots during practice. And after that, he would go to the team practice session and practice with everyone else!

Yes, Kobe Bryant puts in 5–6 hours more than other players every day!

All the Hard Work Pays Off

His commitment to the game was hardcore. On various occasions, he had played with a broken hand, a sprained ankle, a torn shoulder, and a severed lip—without complaining.

And because of this work ethic and commitment, Kobe Bryant ended up winning five NBA championships. He had been included in the All NBA team for a record fifteen times. He had won gold medals for the United States in Olympics twice! He is indeed one of the greats of all time.

Action Summary:

* Be ambitious. Aim to become the best in your field.
* Don't be shackled by what the society expects you to do. Allow your talent to guide you. Go where your talent can be nurtured the most.
* Build on your talent with hard work and commitment. You can become better than others by working harder than others.

Warren Buffett

What Warren Buffett Learns about Investing at the Racetracks

Warren Buffett was known as the best investor the world had ever seen. He was known as the Oracle of Omaha. Over the years, he had invested in companies that had become household names. Companies like Coca-Cola and Gillette. He had turned a lot of people who invested their money with him into millionaires. He himself became a multi-billionaire.

How successful were his investments? He had generated a 20.3% rate of return with his investments since 1964! If you would have invested $10,000 with him in 1964, it would be worth over one hundred and three million dollars in 2014! Just counting the number of zeroes in $103,000,000 makes me dizzy!

Young Warren at the Racetracks

A lot of the success Warren Buffett had with the stock market could be attributed to the lessons he learnt at the racetracks when he was young. Buffett first went to the tracks when he wasn't even a teenager yet with his uncle Frank. Later on, he went to the tracks regularly with his friend Bob Russell, chaperoned by Bob's mother.

But Buffett and his friend were not old enough yet to bet on the races. What were two restless boys meant to do at the racetracks if they couldn't bet? They started selling tip sheets—the “Stable-Boy Selections”! They were soon shut down by the authorities at the racetrack however.

Success at the Racetracks

But Buffett loved the racetracks. Because success on the racetracks depended on two things he was very good at:

1. Collecting information
2. Doing math

When Buffett’s father Howard Buffett was elected to the U.S. House of Representatives and the family moved to Washington D.C., Buffett asked his father for a favor: could he request the Library of Congress to send all the books they had on horse handicapping?

Buffett devoured the books and learnt a lot. He learnt that speed was not everything. A lot of horses did good or bad depending on which jockey was riding them, their position on the racetracks, their recent form, etc.

Buffett then went about systematically testing various betting theories without actually betting any money. He went and bought old racing forms. These were forms that contained various statistical data about past races: horses that entered the races, their past performances and handicap, and the race results. Buffett would do an analysis of the data and try to predict the odds of a horse winning. And then would compare his results with the actual race results.

Because of all these extensive work that Buffett did to educate himself and perfect his systems, he did better than the average person who bet at the racetracks!

Disaster at the Racetracks

But lady luck was fickle. One day, Buffett went to the Charles Town racetrack himself and lost the first race he bet on. To recoup the loss, he bet a bit more on the second race and lost that too. And so he bet a bit more on the third race. He kept on betting and kept on losing. And pretty soon, he found that he had lost $175 in a short afternoon! That's more money than Buffett makes in a week!

This disastrous failure taught him more than his successes however. Buffett learnt the value of patience. He realized that he should not bet on every race. Just bet on races that give significantly better odds. Just bet on races that give undue advantage. Don't bet when behind and under pressure. And remember that there is no need to make money the same way it was lost. Tweak the strategies.

Buffett learnt well from his successes as well as failures and became a legendary stock investor by not ever repeating the mistakes he made as a young bettor at the racetracks!

Action Summary:

- The best way to get an edge over others is to read a lot. Keep on continuously learning and you'll outperform others over the long haul.
- Minimize your risk. Test and validate your ideas.
- Have patience. You don't have to bet on every race. You don't have to work on every new shiny thing that comes to the market. Pick and choose with caution.
- Don't double down on losses. Learn when to quit. You don't have to make it back the way you lost it.

RICHARD FEYNMAN

Richard Feynman's Secret to Tackle and Overcome Burnout

Richard Feynman won the Nobel Prize for physics in 1965. He was weird and eccentric. His hobbies were cracking vaults and playing bongo. But everyone who met him immediately knew that behind the eccentricity was a very very smart human being.

One of the people Feynman impressed was Hans Bethe. Feynman met Bethe at Los Alamos. Both of them were involved in the making of the atomic bomb during World War II. Bethe headed the theoretical division of the Los Alamos lab, and was known as one of the best problem solvers alive. After the war, Bethe got Feynman a job as a professor at Cornell University.

But the journey of being a professor didn't start well for Feynman. The bombing of Hiroshima and Nagasaki depressed him. His wife's death from Hodgkin's lymphoma still haunted him. And soon Feynman found himself in a rut.

The Building of Pressure

Feynman started teaching a course on mathematical methods in physics along with another course on electricity and magnetism. And on top of that he had a few research ideas he wanted to pursue. But he misjudged the amount of work teaching requires. Preparing notes, giving good lectures, and making up good sensible exams all took a lot of time—especially, for a new first time professor. This left Feynman feeling burned out and unable to focus on any research at all.

Reputation of brilliance became burdensome. It built a lot of expectation that Feynman didn't think he could live up to.

The proverbial camel's back was broken when he received an offer letter from the Institute of Advanced Study at Princeton University where other great scientists like Einstein and Kurt Godel and John Von Neumann taught. In fact, the offer Feynman received was for a position even better than Einstein's!

The pressure was too much and physics started disgusting Feynman a bit. He found himself in a rut that lasted for a few months.

The Convoluted Logic

One day Feynman started thinking on it all. He figured that people's expectations were impossible to live up to. Because it was impossible to live up to, he should not be responsible for not meeting their expectations! This convoluted logic freed him!

He started thinking when physics was fun for him. He realized that he enjoyed physics only when he played with it. When he did what he wanted to without caring about the importance of his ideas and research. Without caring if his research would advance the field of nuclear physics or not.

A week or so after this epiphany, Feynman found himself in the cafeteria where he saw a man threw around the plate in the air. The plate had a red Cornell medallion on it. Feynman realized that, when the plate spun, the red medallion spun faster than the wobbling of the plate!

Spinning plates were fun, and solving the puzzle of why a plate rotates faster than it wobbles was something completely unimportant. So Feynman took up the challenge and started deriving formulas and equations of wobbles.

When Feynman shared his plate wobbling work with Hans Bethe, Bethe asked him: “Feynman, that’s pretty interesting, but what’s the importance of it? Why are you doing it?”

And Feynman responded: “Ha! I’m just doing for the fun of it. There is no importance whatsoever.”

But ultimately there was. Because you see, the wobbling equations led Feynman to think about how electron orbits started to move which led him to a few breakthroughs in quantum electrodynamics, because of which he won the Nobel Prize!

Action Summary:

* Don’t let other peoples’ expectations of you bog you down. You are not responsible for what other people think!
* The surest way to get over burn out is to enjoy your work. Make work playful. Do things that you find interesting and entertaining. Ask yourself when you had the most fun with your work, and pursue similar ideas.

Story of the Golden Buddha

Why sharing is important

A nun was searching for enlightenment. To find better focus during daily meditation, she made a statue of Buddha and covered it with a gold leaf. Wherever she went she carried this golden Buddha with her.

Years passed. Still carrying her Buddha, the nun came to live in a small temple in the countryside. This temple had a lot of Buddha statues with their own shrines.

The nun wished to burn incense before her golden Buddha. But she didn't like the idea of the perfume straying to others. So she devised a funnel through which the smoke would ascend only to her statue.

This blackened the nose of her golden Buddha, making it especially ugly.

Action Summary:

- Share good things with others.
- If you liked this book, please give it to your one friend you think will gain from it most.

Gift this Book and make Someone Happier!

"A book is a gift you can open again and again."

– Garrison Keillor

Books make for really special gifts. It helps people learn and grow.

And a book like Genius Biographies—with its small chapters (but big lessons)—makes for a good gift even for people who don't read a lot.

Gift a copy of Genius Biographies to your friend and give them a chance to learn from the lives of the rich and famous.

http://geniusbiographies.com/buy/

Would you like to gift this book to your whole circle of friends or to everyone in your office?

Special discounts on bulk purchases are available:

http://geniusbiographies.com/buy/

The Story of the Vagabonds

In the very early twentieth century, five boys came together to form a mastermind group. Henry, Tom, Harvey, John and Luther met every so often and helped each other plot and plan. They called themselves the Vagabonds!

Not all of these five boys were equal in stature. Some were older and more experienced than others. Some were richer than others. Some were more popular than others. Some worked harder than others. But all five boys had one thing in common. They realized the power of networking, problem solving and sharing of ideas with like-minded folks.

"If you have an apple and I have an apple and we exchange these apples then you and I will still each have one apple. But if you have an idea and I have an idea and we exchange these ideas, then each of us will have two ideas."—George Bernard Shaw

Fast Forward Twenty Years: What Happened to the Vagabond boys?

- Henry Ford became the richest person living.
- Thomas Edison earned the most number of patents any individual ever had.
- Harvey Firestone created the biggest tire manufacturing company.
- John Burroughs became a famous author and naturalist.
- Luther Burbank—a botanist—invented over 800 strains and varieties of plants!

Action Summary:

- Masterminds are powerful. Create or join one to grow your network and keep each other accountable.

Thank you for reading. If you like this book, please review it highly on amazon.